NORTHRUP KING'S

Basic Vegetable Gardening Guide

CONTENTS

Many people have never tasted a fresh vegetable

A wonderfully efficient system brings a year-round supply of uniformly excellent produce to our supermarkets. In size and color and good looks, the mountains of mouth-watering vegetables we see on the produce counters are as fine as modern techniques of truck gardening can supply.

Then why grow your own? There are a number of reasons:

First, to be enjoyed to their fullest, vegetables must be picked and eaten within hours — sometimes minutes — while flavor is at its peak. This is a taste experience many people have never had, and your own home garden makes it yours to enjoy many times over.

Commercial produce must be able to survive mass harvesting methods and bruising journeys to stores, where it must stay appetizing-looking for long periods. To achieve this, growers must of course choose sturdy, hard-skinned varieties that ship well and reach uniform size at a uniform time so that production schedules can be met. Often much tastier varieties must be bypassed because they require individual care that isn't feasible on a mass basis. Or they may lack the attractive appearance so important for supermarket produce.

A garden of your own lets you choose varieties that are frequently tastier, have a more delicate texture, or ripen over a longer period. Also, growing your own vegetables can save you lots of money. In fact, it has been estimated that each hour you spend in your garden can save you $5.00 or more on your grocery bill. And gardening is inflation-proof. The same plot of ground will keep on producing food for you at about the same cost, regardless of how high the price of commercial produce may go.

In addition, there are deep satisfactions in gardening that no one can put a price-tag on. Pressures and tensions disappear, a new serenity prevails as you proceed to "muck about in the soil," as one high-pressure executive puts it.

YOU AND MOTHER NATURE are about to start a great adventure. When you plant a garden you enter a whole new world of discovery and experience. You join a happy group engaged in the fascinating project of harnessing the forces of nature to transform tiny seeds into bountiful crops. Sometimes nature does most of the work, supplying all the warmth and moisture and natural fertilizers plants need. At other times you may have to step in and water or fertilize to remedy problems of drought or poor soil. But however your garden grows, it's an experience you will cherish.

A word of warning, however — gardening is known to be habit-forming. Once you've borne your first proud platter of home-grown delights to your dinner table, you're hooked. You're in for a happier, healthier life from then on!

JUST WHAT THE DOCTOR ORDERED. A recent survey by the American Medical Association revealed that 137,500 of the nation's physicians find relaxation in gardening (over 50% more than the number that play golf).

Make it simple and you make it fun

A small garden can yield big dividends. With a little planning you can have a satisfying garden in a space smaller than many living rooms. Here's an idea for what we call the "Basic Garden" (opposite page). It occupies only 12x15 feet of space, yet it can produce enough fresh vegetables to keep your table supplied bountifully.

The illustration merely shows the minimum space you should devote to different vegetables. You'll want to draw your own garden plan, varying it to fit the space you have available and the kinds of vegetables your family prefers. In planning your garden, keep in mind that some vegetables like cool weather and should be seeded as soon as the danger of frost is past. Beets, carrots, chives, onions, lettuce, peas, radishes, parsley, turnips and rutabagas are in this category. On the other hand, beans, cucumbers, melons and squash like warm weather and should be planted later on, after the soil is warmed up and the weather is pleasantly mild (late spring or early summer).

Peppers, eggplant and tomatoes are usually started indoors (6 to 8 weeks before the outdoor gardening season) then transplanted to the garden when soil and weather conditions permit (see Page 12).

Some rows can serve double duty during the growing season. Lettuce, radishes, beets, carrots, kohlrabi and turnips mature early enough so that after they're harvested the same space may be used to plant late summer and fall crops of the same or different vegetables.

If the only garden plot available to you is one that's shaded part of the day, you'll probably have most success with leaf crops such as lettuce, chard, spinach, mustard or endive. Since the edible part of these is the foliage itself, a partial lack of sun isn't as critical as with vegetables that must develop edible roots or fruit.

Overall, the easiest vegetables to raise are beans, tomatoes, lettuce, radishes, beets, carrots and summer squash.

A basic vegetable garden

Here's how you can grow 13 popular vegetable varieties in a garden measuring only 12x15 feet. Use these suggestions as a starting point for your own plan. Be sure to include any favorite we may have left out.

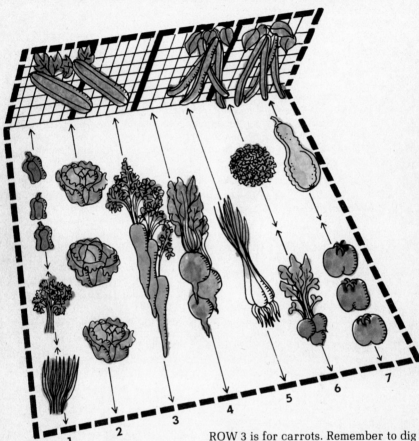

BACK FENCE: Cucumbers and beans are natural climbers, so it's a good idea to plant them near a fence or some sort of laced framework.

ROW 1 includes a clump of flavorsome chives plus a few plants of parsley for tasty garnishes. Fill out the row with peppers.

ROW 2 has your favorite kind of lettuce: head, loose-leaf, romaine, or perhaps a combination.

ROW 3 is for carrots. Remember to dig this row a little deeper than the rest; carrots like plenty of depth to grow in.

ROW 4 is devoted to beets. Both greens and roots are tasty.

ROW 5 is for your choice of onions — the pungent bunching type or the flavorsome bulbing variety.

ROW 6 will supply your salad bowl with radishes and endive.

ROW 7 has tomatoes (stake them or mulch under them) and your favorite type of squash (summer or winter).

WHAT ARE "HYBRID" VARIETIES?

By careful breeding over a number of years, seedsmen have been able to produce vegetables that combine the best features of a number of different varieties. These hybrids, as they are called, usually offer better disease resistance, higher yields or earlier maturities. Hybridizing of seeds is an expensive process, which is why hybrid seeds may cost somewhat more. But the results you'll get usually outweigh the extra investment.

WHICH WAY TO RUN FURROWS:

If you run the rows north and south, each plant will get about the same amount of sunshine, but the advantage isn't really much. It's more important to plan your garden to take advantage of natural surroundings. If your plot has a slope, for instance, be sure to run rows *across* the slope to minimize washing during heavy rains. (A one-foot drop in 50 feet is enough to cause erosion.) Stay away from trees, which create unwanted shade and steal both nutrients and moisture from your growing plants.

PLAN FOR SEQUENTIAL HARVESTS

Try to correlate the size of your family and the number of plantings you make of each vegetable. Limit the number of each type to what you can reasonably expect to consume, unless you plan to can, freeze or give away the surplus. It's also a good idea to make successive plantings, perhaps a week or so apart, to spread the harvest out over a longer period.

YOU NEED VERY FEW TOOLS

You can do a good job on a small garden with these simple tools:
- A spade or fork for digging up the soil;
- A rake for smoothing out clumps, covering seed, removing debris;
- A ball of string and two stakes for marking rows;
- A hoe for making furrows and cultivating; and
- A garden trowel for setting plants, transplanting, close cultivating.

Other basic tools you may gradually acquire include watering and fertilizing equipment (watering can, plastic bucket, hose, soil soaker), wheelbarrow or garden cart, wheeled cultivator, etc.

MIX FLOWERS AND VEGETABLES IF YOU LIKE

There's no reason why you can't plant a few vegetables in your flower garden (or vice versa). Often a planting of parsley, endive, chard, chives or peppers will add a novel touch of beauty to flower beds.

Soil
Sunshine
Moisture

These are the three main factors of success in gardening. Good, loamy soil well laced with nutrients gives your plants the kind of surroundings they like for healthy growth. Adequate sunshine provides the warmth that encourages plant development. Water is important in itself and it also carries food to the growing plants and enables them to utilize it.

YOUR SOIL IS PROBABLY O.K. Generally, any plot of ground that will grow weeds will also grow vegetables. If it turns out that one or more plantings fail to produce a crop because of a soil deficiency, that is the time to take the trouble and spend the money required for a soil analysis. In some states this service is available free; in others a fee is charged, or it may be necessary to employ a private testing laboratory or buy a soil-testing kit of your own. (Check with your county agent or the agricultural college of your state university.)

Sometimes an abnormal pH rating may cause a crop failure. (The pH rating is simply the scientific means of telling you whether your soil is acid or alkaline.) The pH of most garden soils is normally in a range that allows most vegetables to thrive. But occasionally soil may tend toward one extreme or the other. Then it should be corrected to restore the garden to full usefulness.

The solution is easy: If the soil is too acid (low pH rating) just spread lime sparingly and work it into the ground. This will counteract the acidity and bring the pH level up into the normal range. If the soil is too alkaline (high pH rating) add sulphur to bring the acidity level up. (Ask your garden store operator about quantities to use.)

SUNSHINE IS ESSENTIAL

In picking a spot for your garden, keep in mind that most plants require an open sky above them. Don't plant in a spot that's shaded by trees or buildings; direct sunlight for *at least six hours a day* is required for nearly all plants. Putting your garden near trees is also undesirable for another reason: trees will compete with your plants for the available moisture and soil nutrients, and the trees usually win.

KEEP A HEALTHY BALANCE IN YOUR WATER "BANK"

Most vegetables are about 90% water, so you can understand why moisture plays such an important part in gardening success. Generally your garden will require about an inch of water a week throughout the growing season. If Nature cooperates and a gentle one-inch rain falls each week, you'll have no watering problem. But don't count on it. More likely, there will be periods when the sun is blazing hot and no rain falls for weeks. That's when watering becomes vital. (In some areas, such as the Southwest, irrigation is standard practice.)

How to water: There are advantages to each type of watering equipment. A perforated canvas "soaker hose" probably is least wasteful of water, since it lets moisture filter directly down into the soil. But a sprinkler is good, too, since a secondary benefit of watering is to bring down plant temperatures with a refreshing shower.

When to water: Unless you're in a water-short area, the time of day you do your watering doesn't matter particularly. Plants are not likely to be damaged by midday watering as is generally believed. The only disadvantage of watering during the hot part of the day is accelerated evaporation. Incidentally, plants are constantly losing water by transpiration through their leaves, and surface water is also constantly evaporating. That's why it's so important to get a good supply of water down into the soil to a depth where the plants can draw on it through dry spells.

HERE'S WHY SHALLOW WATERING IS BAD

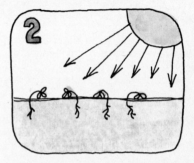

When you water to a depth of only an inch or two, the little rootlets stay up near the surface since they always seek water.

Even a drought of short duration can kill young plants by drying up the soil at the surface. This can happen very quickly.

HERE'S WHY DEEP WATERING IS GOOD

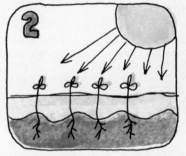

When you soak the ground for a considerable distance down, plants are able to sink deep, healthy roots.

If a drought should occur, the plant's vigorous root system lets it draw on that deep "water bank" and keep on thriving.

HOW MUCH MOISTURE: It's best to water deeply and less frequently. Keep watering until the soil is moist to a depth of eight inches or so. This takes from one to 1½ inches of moisture. How much is that in gallons? Well, your 12x15-foot "mini-garden" will require 120 gallons from your spigot to equal a natural one-inch rainfall.

- *An easy way to judge how much water you're applying is to sink a peanut-butter jar into the soil and use it as a gauge. When the water level in the jar reaches 1½" or so, that should be plenty.*

DON'T PLANT TOO EARLY

It's always a temptation to start planting when the first warm, beautiful days of spring come along. But too often those nice days precede cold snaps that can kill off frost-sensitive plants in minutes. Or the soil may not be dried out enough for successful gardening.

What to do: For warm-season vegetables (see Page 6) wait until the danger of killing frosts is over in your area. Approximate planting times are shown on Pages 16-17. To be on the safe side, especially with tomatoes, peppers and eggplant, get some frost-protective devices for use in case an unusually late freeze develops. (These are little dome-type caps of paper or plastic that create a small "greenhouse" over each plant. Or you may wish to put a wide strip of plastic over an entire row, supporting it with wire hoops every so often. Nail the plastic to 1x2" strips and leave ends open.)

How do you tell when the soil is right for planting? Normally all you have to do is take a handful of soil and squeeze it. If it compresses into a mud ball the soil hasn't dried out enough. If it breaks up into little clumps and dribbles through your fingers, it's O.K. to start planting. Heavy clay soils, of course, tend to compress more easily.

SEEDS OR SEEDLINGS?

It takes quite a long time for some vegetables to mature (celery can take as long as 140 days, for instance). In most parts of the country, the growing season isn't long enough to permit growing all types of vegetables from seed. So it's necessary to give the slower-growing varieties (tomatoes, eggplant, peppers, celery) a head start. This is done by planting the seeds indoors, while it's still cold outside, and letting them grow into fairly good-sized plants before transplanting them into the garden. (Many gardeners delight in being able to harvest their own vegetables long before commercial quantities of produce become available from local growers, and savings over first-of-the-season prices can be quite spectacular.)

HOW TO START TRANSPLANTS

Tomatoes, eggplant and peppers are generally raised via the transplant method, so let's examine how seedlings of these popular favorites are produced.

First of all, since you don't need a huge quantity of soil for transplants, be sure it's of good quality — about 1/3 each of peat, garden soil, and some kind of soil conditioner such as sand, vermiculite or perlite. To kill any harmful organisms in the soil, you might wish to sterilize it. Just put it in the oven at 250° for a half-hour or so. This will prevent the possibility of damping-off or other diseases from developing, and it also kills weed seeds. (In most garden stores you can buy sterilized soil or planting mixture containing just the right elements for transplants.) Let the soil cool before you put it in your flats. Practically any handy

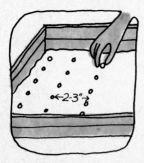

containers will serve as flats — cans, pots, milk cartons, shallow boxes, etc. Be sure they have drainage holes at the bottom. Don't fertilize the transplant soil; this sometimes will encourage too-fast growth and you wind up with tall, spindly plants. Moisten the soil well about two hours before planting your seeds. Scatter seed 1/4" deep in rows 2 or 3 inches apart. Cover with plastic and keep in a warm place (70-80°F). Water only when the soil surface becomes dry to the touch. When seedlings appear, remove the plastic and move the flats to a window, preferably in a somewhat cooler room, where they will get full sunlight. This tends to slow down too-fast top growth and encourages development of a strong, healthy root system.

Water regularly, but avoid sprinkling directly on the seedling leaves.

When the plants are about 2" tall, transplant them into individual pots or into larger flats about 3" apart. About a week before you plan to transplant to the garden, you may wish to cut back on watering and expose the plants to outdoor weather for a few hours daily. This "hardens" the plants gradually so that transplanting isn't so much of a shock to them. Be careful, though. Plants dry out very fast outdoors, especially on windy days. And keep plants out of direct sunshine at first or the tender leaves may burn.

If possible, pick a time just after a rain, or when rain is predicted, to do your transplanting. Cut the seedlings apart in the flats so each one will have a clump of its "nursery" soil around it. Dig a hole for the seedling a bit deeper than it was in the flat, so it sits in a little depression to hold water. Be sure to firm the soil around the roots to eliminate air pockets. (Tomatoes can be planted very deep; they will root all along

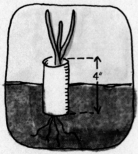

the stem.) Cutworm protection is crucial at this point. Put collars of paper, cardboard, metal, tarpaper or plastic around the plant stems 2" above and 2" below the soil line. The final step is to water well.

Many gardeners prefer to start their transplants in individual "pots" made of moss or peat or other organic matter which are buried, pot and all, when the seedling reaches the proper size. Besides making transplanting easier, this method results in a minimum of transplant shock because roots are not disturbed. Different types are available, including round or square pots, trays, strips, and expanding pellets.

PLANTING SEEDS OUTDOORS

To get the soil ready to receive seeds, dig up your garden plot to a depth of about 8 inches. Break up the big chunks with a spading fork or rake. If your soil is on the light or sandy side, you may wish to apply compost or commercial fertilizer (you'll need about four pounds of commercial fertilizer for your 12x15-foot plot, or about four pints of the liquid type). Pure heavy clay soil can be improved by working humus or compost or sand into the soil.

Rake the surface of the soil well and mark off the rows. (The best way to do this is to drive in small stakes and run string between them.) Make a shallow trench for your seeds with a corner of your hoe or a pointed stick.

Don't plant seeds too deeply; a rule of thumb is three times the smallest width of the seed. Avoid sowing too thickly, especially with the tinier seeds. This just wastes seed and makes thinning more difficult. Try not to plant when the soil is cold and wet — this type of soil often dries into a hard crust that tiny plants have trouble penetrating.

Firm soil over the seeds by treading it down or pressing with the back of your rake. Water the garden well if the soil is dry. *Your garden is now ready for Nature to start working her wonders.*

WHY LATE-SEASON PLANTINGS?

If you see a gardener planting corn or carrots or beets in late June or even July, he's not necessarily a Johnny-come-lately. More likely, he's a *magna-cum-laude*. Because smart gardeners know what a joy it is to be able to harvest crops throughout the fall season. The late-season crops are often bigger, and canning quality is improved over the hot-season vegetables.

FALL GARDENING IS WORK-SAVING GARDENING

A little soil-preparation work in the fall pays big dividends the following spring. If you spend a little time digging up the garden and burying the surface refuse — stalks, dead leaves, weeds — you give Nature a chance to work for you over the winter. First, the garden refuse will be turned into beneficial humus. And second, your spading of the soil accelerates the breaking down of soil-building materials that occurs naturally over the winter freeze period. This means loamier, more workable soil in the spring.

- *A COVER CROP OF RYEGRASS, grown in the fall and turned under, adds plenty of valuable nutrients to the soil.*

ORGANIC GARDENING?   OR CHEMICAL GARDENING?

Reduced to its simplest terms, organic gardening means using only natural means of fertilizing, discouraging weeds and dealing with insects. Chemical gardeners, on the other hand, use essentially man-made compounds for these jobs.

The choice is yours . . . actually there is some good in both methods, and many successful gardeners combine them. Whether the nutrients come from chemical or organic sources makes little difference to the plants themselves — they absorb the nutrients in the same manner whatever their origin.

What is most important is the *balance* of the nutrients. Most fruiting and root crops utilize nitrogen, phosphorus and potash in about a 1-2-1 ratio. This balance can be supplied by a garden fertilizer such as a 5-10-5. (Check the bag; the ratio is on the label.) Scatter four or five pounds of this balanced fertilizer over 100 sq. ft. of garden before planting. A second application may be worthwhile later in the season.

Often gardening failure is due to the lack of one or more of these necessary fertilizer elements. Fruit or roots may fail to develop; the vegetables you do get may be small, malformed or cracked. When this happens it's wise to consult a professional garden supply operator or county agent.

Organic gardeners try to duplicate the natural conditions that produce rich, easily-worked soil. This means providing a desirable environment for the bacteria, earthworms and beneficial insects that inhabit the soil and are constantly working to improve its fertility. Organic matter in the soil harbors many useful micro-organisms which gradually convert nutrients so that plants can absorb them. A properly balanced compost (see page 31) supplies this organic matter, but for faster results you may also want to add a small amount (a pound or so per 100 sq. ft.) of 5-10-5 fertilizer. Peat moss, manure or partially decayed leaves can also be used. Again, best results ensue when some 5-10-5 fertilizer is added.

There is evidence that over the years, organic gardening practices strengthen plant life to the point where it is possibly more resistant to insects and disease. Organic gardeners encourage insect parasites and natural predators to keep the undesirable insect population down. Pyrethrum and rotenone, being organic in origin, are also used by many organic gardeners for insect control. In event of insect invasion that threatens your harvest, prudent use of chemicals is often called for (be sure to read and follow instructions carefully).

MULCHING is one of the important components of organic gardening. By spreading a 2-3" depth of hay, grass clippings, dead leaves, straw, crop residue, etc., the gardener conserves moisture, insulates the soil against heat and cold, prevents run-offs and discourages weed growth. As the mulch itself decays, it adds nutrients to the soil and builds up the organic storehouse below. Mulching underneath tomato or summer squash plants is a good way to keep fruit clean.

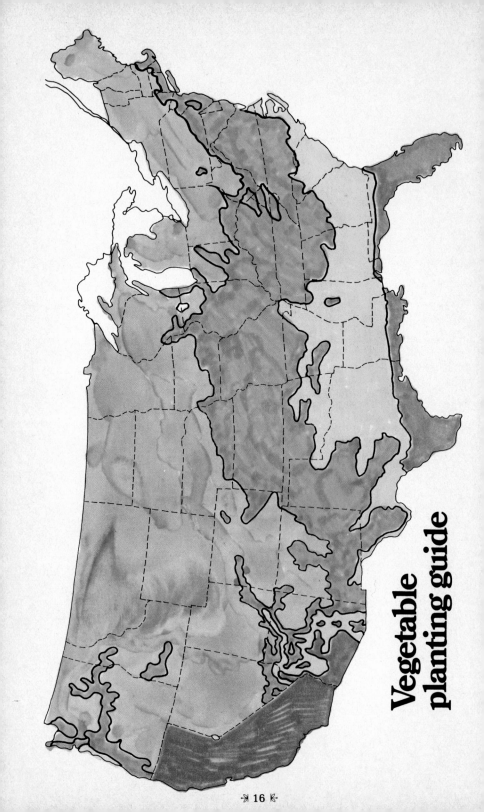

Vegetable
planting guide

This map and accompanying chart are based largely on U. S. Department of Agriculture records showing the average dates of the last killing frosts in various parts of the country. Use this information to plan the planting and harvesting periods for your garden, but remember that these are averages, and individual conditions may vary.

VEGETABLE	PAGE	SUBTROPIC	WARM	MILD	COOL	CALIF.	PLANTING DEPTH	ROW SPACING	FIRST HARVEST	HARVEST LASTS
Beans	18	Apr.-Aug.	Apr.-June	May-June	May-June	Mar.-Aug.	1"	2-3 ft.	8 weeks	Until frost
Beets	20	Jan.-Dec.	Feb.-Oct.	Mar.-July	Apr.-July	Jan.-Dec.	1/2"	15-18"	50-78 days	6 weeks†
Broccoli	22	July-Oct.	Feb.-Mar.	Mar.-Apr.	Mar.-Apr.*	Sep.-Feb.	1/4"	3 ft.	65-70 days	To frost
Brussels sprouts	24	Feb.-May	Feb.-Apr.	Mar.-Apr.*	Mar.-Apr.*	Sep.-Feb.	1/2"	3 ft.	14-20 wks.	Past frost
Carrots	26	Jan.-Dec.	Jan.-Mar.	Mar.-June	Apr.-June	Sep.-May	1/4"	1½-2 ft.	8 weeks	8 weeks†
Chard	28	Jan.-Dec.	Feb.-Sep.	Mar.-Aug.	Apr.-July	Jan.-Dec.	3/4"	1½-2 ft.	8 weeks	To frost
Chives	30	Feb.-May	Mar.-May	Mar.-May	Apr.-June	Mar.-May	1/4"	1½ ft.	8 weeks	To frost
Corn	32	Apr.-June	Mar.-June	May-July	May-July	Mar.-Aug.	1½"	3 ft.	9-12 weeks	10 days
Cucumbers	34	Apr.-June	Apr.-June	Apr.-June	May-June	Mar.-Aug.	1/2"	6 ft.	7 weeks	5 weeks
Eggplant	36	Feb.-Mar.	Feb.-Apr.	Mar.-May*	Apr.-May*	Mar.-May	1/4"	3-4 ft.	10-14 wks.	To frost
Endive	36	July-Sep.	Aug.-Sep.	Mar.-May	Apr.-June	Jan.-Dec.	1/4"	2-3 ft.	10-12 weeks	7 weeks
Lettuce	38	Jan.-Dec.	Aug.-May	Mar.-June	Apr.-June	Sep.-May	1/4"	15"	6 weeks	6 weeks†
Mustard	40	Feb.-May	Feb.-May	Mar.-June	May-July	Mar.-Aug.	1/4"	1½-2 ft.	40-50 days	2 weeks
Okra	42	Apr.-June	Apr.-June	Apr.-June	May-june*	Mar.-May	1/2-3/4"	3 ft.	55-60 days	To frost
Onions	44	Dec.-Mar.	Dec.-Apr.	Feb.-May	Mar.-June	Sep.-May	1/2"	18"	Variable	—
Parsley	46	Jan.-Dec.	Jan.-June	Feb.-June	Mar.-June	Jan.-Dec.	1/4"	1½-2 ft.	10 weeks	To frost
Parsnips	47	Mar.-June	Feb.-June	Apr.-June	May-June	Dec.-May	1/2"	1½-2 ft.	14-17 wks.	Past frost
Peas	48	Jan.-May	Jan.-Apr.	Feb.-May	Mar.-June	Sep.-May	1½"	2-3 ft.	9 weeks	2 weeks†
Peppers	50	Feb.-Mar.	Feb.-Apr.	Mar.-May*	Mar.-May*	Mar.-May*	1/4"	3 ft.	9 weeks	To frost
Potatoes	52	Jan.-Dec.	Feb.-Oct.	Mar.-Apr.	Apr.-May	Jan.-Dec.	5"	2½-3 ft.	100 days	To frost
Pumpkin	52	Apr.-June	Apr.-June	Apr.-June	May-June	Sep.-May	1"	8-10 ft.	14-17 wks.	To frost
Radishes	53	Jan.-Dec.	Feb.-Oct.	Mar.-Aug.	Apr.-July	Sep.-May	1/4"	1-2 ft.	3-6 weeks	1-2 weeks†
Squash, Summer	54	Apr.;june	Apr.;june	Apr.;june	May-june	Mar.-Aug.	1"	4-6 ft.	60 days	To frost
Squash, Winter	54						1"	6-8 ft.	100 days	"
Tomatoes	56	Jan.-Mar.	Feb.-Mar.	Mar.-May*	Mar.-May*	Mar.-May*	1/4"	3-4 ft.	9-12 weeks	To frost
Turnips	58	Jan.-Feb.	Jan.-Mar.	Feb.-Apr.	Mar.-May	Jan.-Dec.	1/2"	1-2 ft.	6-10 weeks	3 weeks†

*Transplants recommended.
†Following harvest, space may be used for late planting of carrots, beets or bush beans.

BEANS

Snap beans were being cultivated by the Indians at the time Columbus arrived in America. They have since become popular over most of the globe.

Your bean plants will probably yield a bigger harvest than you expect; this is a vegetable that produces in quantity over a long picking season. Pole beans mature a little later than bush-type beans, but require less garden space and are easier to pick.

One pound of snap beans serves 3 to 4 people. They are simple to prepare; pop them into boiling water and simmer for 8 to 10 minutes after the water returns to a boil. Test for tenderness. For a real treat, cook them with a tablespoon or two of minced onion, green pepper or parsley.

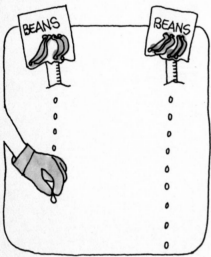

PLANT in smooth, lump-free soil, spacing seeds about 1½" apart in furrows 2 to 3 feet apart. Cover 1" deep and press soil firmly down.

CULTIVATE soon after seedlings appear (7 to 10 days). Thin to about 3" apart when plants are 2" high.

CANNING: Wash and drain young, tender beans fresh from the garden. Trim the ends off, cut into pieces and follow usual canning procedure.

FREEZING: Prepare as for canning, then scald for three minutes and freeze.

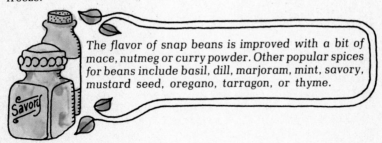

The flavor of snap beans is improved with a bit of mace, nutmeg or curry powder. Other popular spices for beans include basil, dill, marjoram, mint, savory, mustard seed, oregano, tarragon, or thyme.

HOW MUCH TO PLANT: Figure on about six feet of row per person. Plant more if you plan to can or freeze.

WHEN TO PLANT: Wait until frost danger is past. Beans are super-sensitive to cold — they can be killed by the slightest touch of frost.

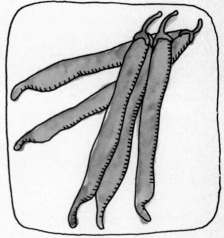

DON'T WORK ON YOUR BEANS if they're wet; that's when bean diseases are usually spread.

HARVEST as soon as the pods reach a good size and seeds are still tender. If allowed to become overly mature, pods will be tough and fibrous. Keep pods picked and the plant will continue to bear.

BEETS

Here's a favorite of gardeners everywhere, and no wonder — beets are easy to grow and delicious to eat. Beet aficionados especially cherish the wonderful flavor of young, half-grown beets — a treat your home garden will produce in quantities. Roman epicures had their favorite beet recipes as long as 1800 years ago.

Beet greens are an unbelievably good source of Vitamin A. In fact, just half a cup of cooked beet greens will give you twice the recommended daily minimum of Vitamin A. And if you serve the greens uncooked (they're delicious in salads) you'll find they're packed with not only Vitamin A, but also Vitamin C and Vitamin G.

There's a trick to preparing beets. Don't cut the stems too close; leave an inch of the stems on, or you'll find that the beet roots "bleed" as they're being cooked. Simmer whole beets in salted water for 30 to 45 minutes, then pour cold water over them and slip the skins off. Serve them whole, sliced or diced.

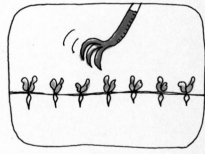

PLANT in rows 15" to 18" apart. Scatter seed ½" apart, cover ½" deep and press soil down firmly. You should see plants emerging in 7 to 10 days.

CULTIVATE while both your beets and the weeds are small. Weeds will fight for moisture and nutrients, so get rid of them.

CANNING: Pack boiled, skinned, trimmed beets into hot jars, adding a teaspoon of salt to each quart. Cover with boiling water and process in usual way.

PICKLING: Recipes for pickled beets abound, many of them handed down for generations. The home-grown flavor of your beets will add a new dimension to this old favorite.

FREEZING: Chill cooked beets, peel and cut as desired. Follow normal freezing procedure.

- *Beets will usually keep all winter if stored in a cool, (35-40°F) moist place, especially in sand.*

- *Beets are delicious with just a touch of allspice, bay leaves, dill, caraway seed, cloves, ginger, mustard seed, savory, or thyme.*

- *Each beet seed is really a multiple seed, which is why it grows so many plants. This is also the reason beets require such careful thinning.*

HOW MUCH TO PLANT: Figure on a six-foot row of beets for each member of the family. (A packet of seeds should make one row about 25 feet long.) Plant more if you plant to pickle, can or freeze.

WHEN TO PLANT: Beets will grow well even in cool weather, so try to get yours planted as early as possible after the soil becomes workable in the spring. Plant another crop in midsummer for fall harvesting.

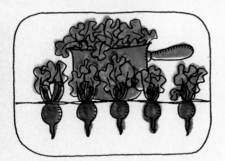 

THIN OUT plants when they are 1½" high. Leave 1½" between them. Thin again at 4 or 5 inches, leaving 3" between them. Don't discard thinnings — they are most delicious, particularly the tiny "baby beets."

HARVEST when your beets are not more than 3" across. (This should take 50 to 78 days.) Beyond this size they have usually passed their peak of flavor.

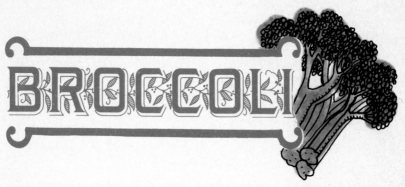

BROCCOLI

"Broccoli" is an Italian word taken from the Latin *brachium*, which means an arm or branch. Actually broccoli is the partially-developed cluster of flower buds of a plant related to cauliflower. It originated in the Mediterranean area and was highly prized by the Romans. Broccoli has only become popular across America in the past half-century or so; before that only a few epicures in eastern seaboard cities grew and appreciated it.

Broccoli is one of our most nutritious foods; its Vitamin C content is very high and it is a good source of iron, calcium and Vitamin A. There are many ways to serve broccoli; a popular method is to simmer bud clusters plus a few inches of stalk in very little water and serve with your favorite butter sauce.

CANNING: Wash and slice into the size you like and proceed with normal canning procedure. (Broccoli often develops a somewhat strong flavor when canned and may go off color.)

FREEZING: Wash and trim freshly-picked broccoli, discarding any heads that blossom. Soak for ½ hour in salt brine to drive out any insects. Blanch for four minutes, chill, and freeze.

HOW MUCH TO PLANT: About six broccoli plants per person will produce an ample supply. Plant more if you plan to can or freeze.

WHEN TO PLANT: Sow seed in open ground as soon as the danger of heavy freeze is past. In colder areas, you can have an earlier crop by starting transplants about 4 to 5 weeks before outdoor planting begins. Broccoli takes from 65 to 70 days to mature from seed.

HARVESTING TIP: Take about 3-4 inches of the edible stem with the center head; this seems to stimulate further production of side shoots you can pick later on.

- *The flavor of broccoli is improved with a touch of caraway seed, dill, mustard seed, or tarragon.*

PLANT seeds sparingly in rows 3 feet apart. Cover seeds ¼" deep and press soil firmly over row. (In short-season areas, you may wish to start plants indoors and transplant, spacing plants 18" to 24" apart in rows 3 feet apart.)

CULTIVATE soon after the seedlings begin to appear (in 6 to 10 days) and keep weeds down thereafter.

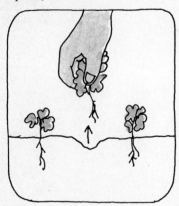

THIN gradually until plants are 3 feet apart for healthy growth.

HARVEST while the heads (bud clusters) are still hard and green, but before the florets begin to separate. If kept picked and not allowed to flower, the plant will keep producing until late fall or freeze-up.

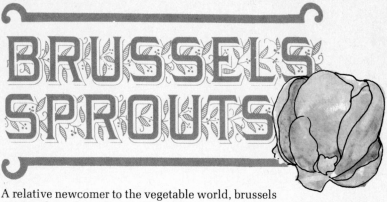

BRUSSELS SPROUTS

A relative newcomer to the vegetable world, brussels sprouts have been known for a mere 400 years or so. This prolific member of the cabbage family first became popular in Belgium's capital city, hence its name.

As the plant grows, it forms quantities of little walnut-sized "cabbages" along its stem. These sprouts have a unique taste that has been described as like a combination of cauliflower, broccoli and cabbage.

QUICK VEGETABLE

Brussels sprouts are ready to eat after about 8 minutes of boiling. Use very little water. For super-fast preparation, a minute in a pressure cooker suffices. Do not overcook.

Cream and cheese sauces go well with the distinctive flavor of brussels sprouts; they are also good cooked with butter and onions.

Brussels sprouts need a long, cool growing season. Except in mild areas, they should be started indoors (see page 12) and moved out into the garden when plants are 6" in height and all frost danger is past. Apply cutworm safeguards (see page 13) and water well.

CANNING: Soak peeled sprouts in salt water for ten minutes or so, then drain and boil 3 minutes before completing usual canning procedure. (Canned brussels sprouts often become discolored and somewhat strong-flavored.)

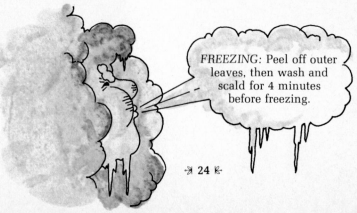

FREEZING: Peel off outer leaves, then wash and scald for 4 minutes before freezing.

HOW MUCH TO PLANT: An 8-foot row for each person will be ample. Plant more if you plan to can or freeze.

SET TRANSPLANTS 1½ feet apart in rows 3 feet apart. Pick off top few leaves.

BREAK OFF lower leaves when sprouts begin to form; this helps the buds along.

HARVEST ANYTIME after sprouts (buds) reach 1" or so in diameter. Begin with lower sprouts and work up plant. Sprouts are even more delicious after a light frost, and the plant will continue to produce until a really heavy freeze.

CARROTS

This is a vegetable that has had its ups and downs through the centuries. The early Greeks valued the carrot for its medicinal qualities and touted it as a stomach tonic. In 17th-century England the carrot was a familiar farm crop, and it was carried by early explorers to the New World, where it was grown in both the Jamestown and the Plymouth settlements. At one time carrots were chopped and dried for use as a coffee substitute.

Later the carrot appears to have lost favor and for many years Americans considered it a fit food only for horses. But in the last half-century it has again become popular for its fine eating qualities and nutritional benefits. The carrot's extraordinary richness in Vitamin A has made it a favorite with health enthusiasts. Carrot-eating is said to be especially beneficial to night vision. It is probably the easiest vegetable to raise, since it has very few natural enemies and requires only simple care.

Be sure to prepare the soil deeply for carrots — they need plenty of room to develop underground or they may become stunted or malformed. Drought and poor soil can create strong flavor.

Besides the popular peas-and-carrots combination, carrots also go well with lima beans and onions. Fresh, young carrots cook in less than 20 minutes and are a valuable addition to soups and stews. Baked carrots is a popular dish, and very simple to prepare:

Cut washed and scraped carrots lengthwise and place in a greased casserole. Add ¼ cup hot water and dot with 2 to 3 tablespoons butter or margarine. Sprinkle with salt and pepper. Cover and bake in 375° oven until tender (about 45 minutes).

CANNING: Wash and scrape freshly-picked carrots. Slice, dice larger carrots and boil 3 minutes. Follow with normal canning procedure.

FREEZING: Wash and peel trimmed carrots. Cut larger sizes into slices, scald and freeze in usual way.

- *Carrots store well at 35-40°F, preferably at high humidity or covered with dry sand.*

HOW MUCH TO PLANT: About 6-8 feet of garden row per person will produce a season-long supply. Plant more if you plan to can or freeze. If you'd like to have a supply of tender young carrots for fall use, sow carrots in mid-season. You'll get quantities of small finger-size carrots that are delicious and good for winter storage.

WHEN TO PLANT: Carrots can tolerate light frost, so plant them anytime from early spring on. Prolonged hot weather may cause lower yields and stronger flavor in carrots.

PLANT in a sheltered location on mellow loam. Scatter seeds ½" apart in rows 1½ to 2 feet apart. Make successive plantings every two weeks until mid-season.

CULTIVATE around the seedlings soon after they start to appear (in about two weeks). Don't let weeds get the jump on you; carrots have trouble competing with them. Cultivate regularly, but not too deeply.

THIN OUT plants when third leaf appears and plants are about 2 to 3" high. Thin two or three times lightly rather than all at once; plants should be about 2-3" apart finally.

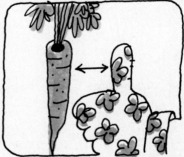

HARVEST should begin as soon as the roots are thumb-size or larger. Carrots have their best flavor when not more than 2" in diameter. Pull largest plants first to give smaller ones growing room.

CHARD

Swiss Chard is a beet-like plant that doesn't develop the familiar beet root. It has been a well-known crop in Europe since about the time of Aristotle. A very prolific plant, chard is increasing in popularity as an all-around vegetable. Unlike spinach, it tolerates summer heat well. Its large leaves can be harvested from growing plants without harming them. Cooked like spinach, eaten raw in salads, or used as a "lettuce" filler for sandwiches, chard is tasty and nutritious. The stalk can be prepared like asparagus.

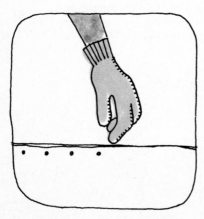

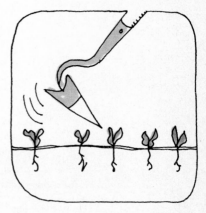

PLANT as soon as frost danger is past in the spring, preferably in rich, well-drained, sandy-loamy soil. Scatter seed sparingly in rows 1½ to 2 feet apart, covering seed about ¾" deep. Press soil firmly over seed.

CULTIVATE soon after seedlings appear (in 7 to 10 days).

CANNING: Choose only smaller, tender stems. Wash thoroughly and heat until wilted. Cut through several times and follow usual canning procedure.

FREEZING: Pull leafy part from stalk, wash thoroughly, scald for three minutes, chill, and follow usual freezing method.

HOW MUCH TO PLANT: About 6 feet of row per person will be ample. Plant more if you plan to can or freeze.

HARVESTING TIP: Cut with a sharp knife at the base of the stem and you won't disturb the root or crown. Young leaves measuring 6 to 8 inches have the best flavor.

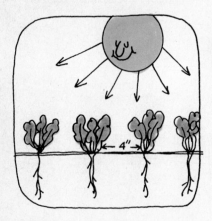

THIN when plants are about 3-4" tall so that plants are 4 to 6 inches apart.

HARVEST as you wish throughout the growing period. Pick individual leaves, or cut leaf stalks carefully just above ground and new growth will continue.

CHIVES

One of many relatives of the onion, chives are both tasty and attractive in your garden and as a wintertime houseplant. The dainty chive plants have slender, hollow green leaves and clusters of charming lavender flowers. Many travelers report seeing chives growing wild in Greece and Italy.

Chives may be harvested at any time, and make a piquant addition to salads, stews, soups, cheese and egg dishes. Sprinkle chopped chives on a warm loaf of French bread for a real treat!

A hardy perennial, chives will continue to come up season after season.

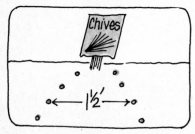

PLANT in early spring about ¼" deep in rows 1½ feet apart. Press soil firmly over seeds.

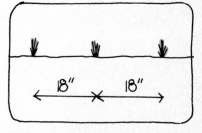

THIN when plants are 3" high to leave one plant every 18" or so.

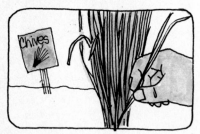

HARVEST leaves when you need them. Plant will continue to grow.

DIG UP a clump and bring inside the house in the fall. Placed in a sunny window, it will produce for you all winter.

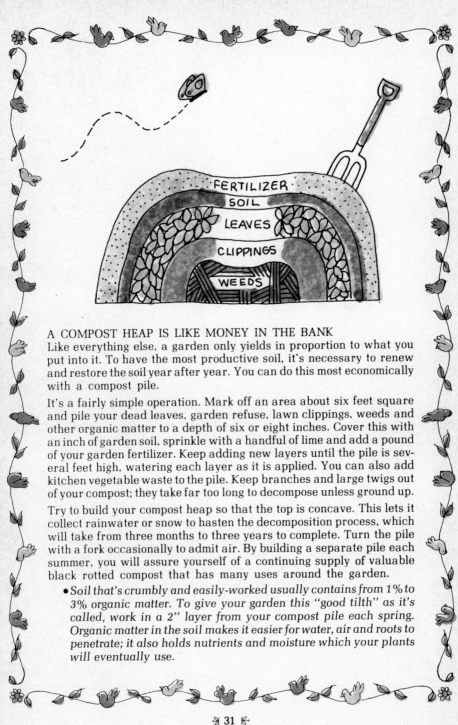

FERTILIZER
SOIL
LEAVES
CLIPPINGS
WEEDS

A COMPOST HEAP IS LIKE MONEY IN THE BANK

Like everything else, a garden only yields in proportion to what you put into it. To have the most productive soil, it's necessary to renew and restore the soil year after year. You can do this most economically with a compost pile.

It's a fairly simple operation. Mark off an area about six feet square and pile your dead leaves, garden refuse, lawn clippings, weeds and other organic matter to a depth of six or eight inches. Cover this with an inch of garden soil, sprinkle with a handful of lime and add a pound of your garden fertilizer. Keep adding new layers until the pile is several feet high, watering each layer as it is applied. You can also add kitchen vegetable waste to the pile. Keep branches and large twigs out of your compost; they take far too long to decompose unless ground up.

Try to build your compost heap so that the top is concave. This lets it collect rainwater or snow to hasten the decomposition process, which will take from three months to three years to complete. Turn the pile with a fork occasionally to admit air. By building a separate pile each summer, you will assure yourself of a continuing supply of valuable black rotted compost that has many uses around the garden.

- *Soil that's crumbly and easily-worked usually contains from 1% to 3% organic matter. To give your garden this "good tilth" as it's called, work in a 2" layer from your compost pile each spring. Organic matter in the soil makes it easier for water, air and roots to penetrate; it also holds nutrients and moisture which your plants will eventually use.*

CORN

Corn originated somewhere in the fertile lowlands east of the Andes Mountains in South America and was raised by the Indians long before white explorers appeared. The corn the Indians grew had red, white, yellow and black kernels on each ear. Later, all-white ears were developed and became quite popular. These were succeeded by all-yellow ears in most areas, although white corn is still popular in the South.

Cooking sweet corn is very simple — just simmer it for 8 minutes, lather on butter and salt to taste. But to enjoy that just-picked flavor, you have to work fast between picking and cooking. The real corn enthusiasts specify an exact procedure to follow:

(1) Bring pot of water to a boil on the range.

(2) While water is boiling, walk to your garden and inspect ears still on the stalk, selecting those at just the right stage of milkiness and tip fill. Choose ears with dark green husks; those with yellow or whitish husks are too old.

(3) Pick the prime ears and run — do not walk — back to the kitchen, where the ears are immediately husked and plunged into the boiling water.

This may sound exaggerated, and it is. But it is a fact that sweet corn starts losing its flavor the moment it's picked. The corn's delicious sugars begin turning into starch immediately — only in those magic minutes right after picking is corn at its gastronomical peak.

CANNING: Husk freshly-picked ears and remove silk. After washing, sort cobs for size (or cut kernels from cobs) and follow usual canning procedure.

FREEZING: Husk freshly-picked ears and remove silk. Blanch for 8 or 10 minutes, then chill thoroughly in cold water and freeze. If you prefer whole-kernel corn, blanch cobs for 4½ minutes before cutting the kernels off.

HOW MUCH TO PLANT: A 25-foot row for each person will produce ample supplies. Plant more if you plan to can or freeze.

WHEN TO PLANT: Normally home gardeners wait until all danger of frost is past to plant corn. But the delights of early corn are such that many risk earlier plantings. See map and chart on Pages 16-17 for planting suggestions.

PLANT in solid blocks rather than long rows for better pollination. Drop two seeds close together every 20 inches in rows 3 feet apart. Cover seeds 1½'' deep and firm soil well.

CULTIVATE soon after the first seedlings appear (in about 7 to 10 days).

HARVEST when ear is blocky to the tip (not tapered or sharp) and filled out with kernels that spurt milky juice when punctured. Cook or refrigerate the ears immediately after picking.

CUCUMBERS

If you like cucumbers, you're in some exalted company. The Emperor Tiberius was so crazy about them that he harried the imperial gardeners into developing artificial methods of growing cucumbers out of season so that he could enjoy them daily the year round. Charlemagne grew cucumbers in his 9th-century gardens. And Columbus thought so highly of them that he brought cucumber seed to Haiti for planting in 1494.

Eaten raw, cucumbers have a delightful flavor. They are sliced or diced in salads, cut lengthwise into sticks, used in sandwiches, or prepared in a variety of other ways. Many people enjoy them sliced with vinegar and salt and pepper; sour cream dressing is also a very popular accompaniment.

PICKLING: There are dozens of ways of pickling cucumbers — whole, sliced, in chips or chunks, sour, sweet, spiced, unspiced. Use only the small-to-medium sizes and be sure to pickle within a day or so of harvesting for best flavor.

PLANT in a warm, sunny spot. To save garden space, plant alongside a fence or trellis. Plant seeds 4" apart, or in hills of 6 to 8 seeds, each hill 4 to 6 feet from the next. Cover seeds ½" deep and firm soil over them.

CULTIVATE soon after seedlings appear (in about a week). Cultivate shallow and often to avoid cutting plant roots.

> *HARVESTING TIPS: If you are grow-ing cucumbers for pickling, harvest them when they're still small; if for table use, allow them to grow bigger. Never lift the vines up high when you are harvesting; this tends to tear the vines and reduce their yields. Just roll the vines over, pick the fruit and let the vines roll back into place. Incidentally, you won't get a cucum-ber from each blossom that you see on your vines. Only female flowers bear fruit; the males are just for pollination.*

HOW MUCH TO PLANT: One or two hills per person will supply plenty of cucumbers for raw eating and pickling.

WHEN TO PLANT: Cucumbers are especially susceptible to frost, so wait until late spring when soil is warm and frost danger is past.

THIN when seedlings are one to two inches tall. Do it in stages rather than all at once, until you have plants about one foot apart (or 3 plants per hill.).

HARVEST regularly, several times a week, even if you don't intend to use the fruit. This stimulates the plant to longer and more abundant production. Inspect plants often for cucumber beetles and pick them off or dust the plants.

EGGPLANT

Sliced, breaded and fried, eggplant has a pleasant, mild flavor. It also combines well with other vegetables in casseroles. Inventive cooks find it an ideal background dish for delicate sauces and seasonings.

PLANTING: For earliest and largest crops, use transplants (see page 13) started at least 8 weeks beforehand. Wait until weather is thoroughly warmed up before transplanting, and protect seedlings against cutworms (page 13).

HARVESTING: Once the first fruits have set and are starting to develop, pick off any further blossoms that appear. When the fruits are about 4'' in diameter and still glossy, they're at their peak.

CANNING: Cut washed and pared eggplant into slices or cubes, let stand in cold water for an hour or so. Then drain and boil for 5 minutes. Follow with normal canning procedure.

FREEZING: Peel, slice, and immerse in salt water to prevent darkening. Then scald 4½ minutes in salt water, chill, drain, and package.

ENDIVE

This vitamin-rich addition to salads is also used in flavoring soups and stews. *Curly endive* has narrow, ragged-edge leaves which are dark green and somewhat bitter at the outer edges of the plant. The inner leaves, however, are yellowish-white, tender and delicious. Another variety, *Batavian endive,* (also called *escarole*) has broader leaves that do not curl. The heart leaves blanch to a creamy white and have a fine flavor. Both are good sources of Vitamin A and also contain Vitamins B, C, and G.

Endive grows best in cool weather; too much exposure to high temperatures will tend to make it less desirable in flavor. Sow endive in early spring after frosts are past, or plant a fall crop in midsummer. Fairly rich, moist soil is most desirable. Sow seed ¼'' deep in rows 2 to 3 feet apart. Firm soil over row. Thin to 6- or 8-inch spacing when seedlings are 1½-2'' high. When plants are well along, outer leaves are sometimes tied together loosely with rubber bands or plant ties so that inner leaves become blanched and flavorsome.

HERBS

A GARDEN OF HERBS near the kitchen door is often the secret of those subtle flavors attained by gourmet cooks. Herbs have a unique power to bring out the best in foods when used with discretion.

You may wish to experiment with a few plantings of herbs before deciding to plant a full herb garden. You're most likely to be successful if you choose the more easily grown varieties.

Sweet basil is one. It germinates in a week or so, has a pleasant clove-like aroma and taste. Used in soups, stews, omelets and salads.

Broad-leaf sage is another possibility. It takes longer to come up — two weeks or so — and has a flavor that is quite strong and pungent. Popular as a tea, sage is also used in meats, dressings, gravies and cheeses.

Summer savory is another favorite; it germinates in about ten days, and the entire plant is pleasantly aromatic. Used in salads and dressings; especially popular as a flavoring for snap beans.

Sweet marjoram is one of the more useful herbs, adding a piquancy to everything from sausage to fish dishes. This is also a slow-grower, and often requires careful nurturing.

English thyme is one of the most familiar herbs and a pleasant addition to soups, salads, dressings, omelets and gravies. It germinates in ten days or so, has such a pronounced flavor that a little goes a long way.

Dill germinates in 10 or 12 days, matures in six weeks. For top flavor, harvest when immature seeds form umbrella-shaped clusters. They are used in making pickles and sauerkraut, can be sprinkled on salads or used in soups and gravies. The fresh leaves are also chopped and used sparingly on salads, in soups and stews.

Make sure you plant your herbs in the sunniest part of your garden. Well-drained soil is also a must.

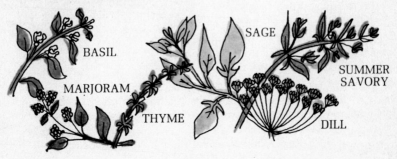

BASIL

SAGE

SUMMER SAVORY

MARJORAM

THYME

DILL

LETTUCE

Popular throughout the civilized world since the earliest times, lettuce was one of the first vegetables introduced to the Western Hemisphere by Columbus. Of all the vegetables grown in home gardens, lettuce probably offers the most opportunity for experimentation and discovery. There are three basic types:

The familiar heading type (Iceberg, for instance) found in supermarkets is adequate for filling a salad bowl, but the flavor is unexceptional and it is not as easy to grow in many areas as the other types.

Romaine (or Cos) was a favorite among the early Romans, hence its name. This type forms a rosette of elongated leaves with a distinctive flavor highly valued by gourmet cooks.

Loose-leaf varieties (Grand Rapids, Black-Seeded Simpson) are easiest to grow, earliest to harvest and richest in vitamins.

Lettuce does best when the weather is cool; hot weather causes it to grow too fast and become somewhat bitter in taste. Leaves of the non-heading types can be harvested at any time; this will not affect the plant's growth. The thinnings also make delicious additions to your salads.

PLANT in early spring as soon as soil can be worked. Be sure soil is smooth and lump-free.

SCATTER SEED sparingly in rows 15" apart. Cover ¼" deep and firm soil over row.

THIN OUT the young plants to 4" apart (loose-leaf varieties) or 8" apart (heading varieties).

HARVEST loose-leaf types at different stages of development; you'll enjoy sampling flavor and texture variations.

MUSTARD

Vitamin-rich mustard originated in northwest India and has since spread over the globe. It is an easily-grown crop, heat-tolerant and useful both cooked and in salads.

Use your mustard greens soon after picking; they will lose nearly a quarter of their Vitamin C content and start wilting within 24 hours unless refrigerated. Use the young, tender leaves in salads; the mature leaves should be cooked in very little water. About 20 to 30 minutes of simmering is required.

CANNING: Choose only smaller, tender-stemmed leaves. Wash thoroughly and heat until wilted. Cut through several times and follow usual canning method.

FREEZING: Pull leafy part from stalk, wash thoroughly, scald for 3 minutes, chill, and freeze.

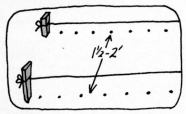

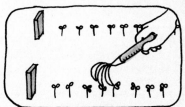

PLANT in any moderately rich, well-drained soil. Scatter seed thinly ¼ " deep in rows 1½ to 2 feet apart. Press soil firmly over seeds.

CULTIVATE soon after the seedlings emerge (in 4 to 5 days). Continue cultivating as long as weeds appear.

THIN to 6 inches apart in row. Thin out gradually rather than in one sweep.

HARVEST the leaves while they are young and tender; more will usually sprout to give you a continuous supply for weeks.

KEEP PICKING OFF the mature fruit of summer squash, cucumbers, broccoli and most beans even if you don't plan to use them. This tends to keep the plant producing over a longer period.

DON'T OVERCOOK YOUR VEGETABLES. To get the most in flavor and eating enjoyment from your vegetables, it's best to undercook rather than overcook them. If the instructions say "Boil for 20 minutes," bring the water to a boil and then simmer for 20 minutes. Overcooking makes vegetables soggy and destroys their attractive color. Incidentally, to retain a maximum of color in your vegetables, simmer them in lots of water, preferably with no lid on the pot.

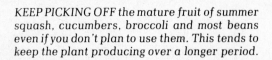

Q. *What is the difference between humus and compost?*
A. Humus is what you have when the organic matter on your compost pile has decayed to a point where it is a black, crumbly mass. All organic matter, after it is buried, will in time decompose into humus. Your compost pile provides you with a "bank" of organic matter that has been partially or fully converted into humus, depending upon how long the compost pile has been working.

Q. *Should I build a fence around my garden?*
A. If you have problems with unwanted visitors, this might be a good idea. A fence also increases the usable area of your garden. Plant your pole beans, tall peas and tomatoes close to the fence so they can climb up it. Cucumbers and squash are climbers also.

Q. *How effective is manure as a fertilizer?*
A. A ton of manure has only the nutritional value of about a 25-pound sack of commercial fertilizer, and manure may have weed seeds or disease organisms in it. But manure is desirable for the organic matter it contains, which will turn to valuable humus as it decays in the soil.

A 25x25-FOOT PLOT OF GROUND has about 40 pounds of weed seeds in it. This is why regular cultivation is necessary through early summer.

OKRA

An import from Africa, okra is an important ingredient of many Creole dishes and was probably introduced to this country by the French settlers of Louisiana. Okra is rarely served alone except in some parts of the South; it is most often used to make a gumbo for thickening soups.

Be sure to harvest your okra before the pods become too old and tough. Gardeners who discover the flavor of the tender pods quickly become okra enthusiasts. Baby pods boiled ten minutes or so are delicious, especially with Hollandaise sauce. Okra is a good source of Vitamin G and also contains amounts of Vitamins B and C. Be sure to use utensils of aluminum when cooking okra — iron, copper or brass pots tend to cause a harmless discoloration of the okra.

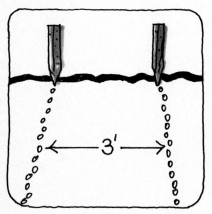

PLANT in rich, warm, sunny soil. Scatter seed thinly in rows 3 feet apart, covering ½" to ¾" deep. Press soil firmly over seeds.

CULTIVATE soon after seedlings appear (in 15 to 20 days). Continue cultivating to keep weeds down.

CANNING: Wash and drain young, tender pods from which stem and blossoms have been removed. Boil a couple of minutes and follow usual canning method.

FREEZING: Prepare okra as for canning, then scald 3 to 4 minutes and chill. Freeze in usual way.

HOW MUCH TO PLANT: About six okra plants will supply one person adequately. Plant more if you plan to can or freeze.

WHEN TO PLANT: Wait until weather and soil are thoroughly warm. In northern latitudes it's a good idea to start transplants indoors and move them outside when you're sure the danger of frost is past.

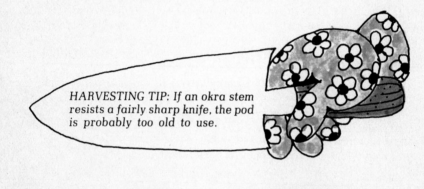

HARVESTING TIP: If an okra stem resists a fairly sharp knife, the pod is probably too old to use.

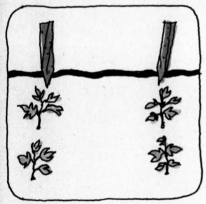

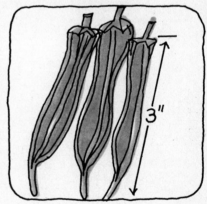

THIN plants gradually when they reach 2 to 3 inches in height. Continue thinning until you have from 1 to 1½ feet between plants.

HARVEST pods while they are still young and tender (not more than 3 inches long).

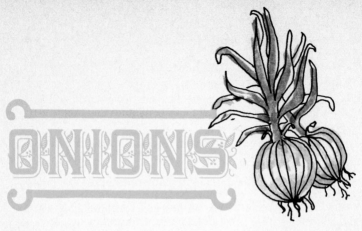

ONIONS

The pungent, flavorsome onion has been adding zip to meals since man's earliest history. Onions were first cultivated in middle Asia and later became a favorite food of the Egyptians. The Bible tells how the Israelites, during their wanderings in the wilderness, recalled fondly the onions, leeks and garlic they had enjoyed in Egypt. Introduced to America by Spanish explorers, the onion was a mainstay of early colonists' diet.

Onions are delicious eaten raw, boiled, stuffed, sauteed, scalloped, french fried, broiled, baked, or added to soups, stews and gravies. Since most onions store well, canning or freezing is usually unnecessary.

Onions are raised either from seed or from "sets". The latter are small, immature bulbs started from seed the preceding year. The big, mild Spanish onion popular on hamburgers requires a longer growing season, so this type is usually started via transplants (see page 13).

BUNCHING ONIONS

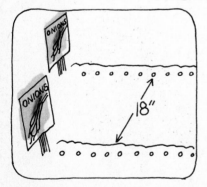

PLANT in early spring as soon as the soil can be worked. Sow generously at ½" depth in rows 18" apart, pressing soil firmly over seeds.

HARVEST at will. The first seedlings will appear in 8 to 12 days, after which you should thin plants to a 1" spacing.

Many people enjoy onions in their early green stage; all varieties can be picked and eaten early, and some (White Lisbon, for instance) are raised especially for use as green or "bunching" onions.

Bulbing onions raised from seed usually have better storage quality than those raised from sets.

HOW MUCH TO PLANT: About six feet of row will supply one person. Plant more if you plan to store a quantity.

● *Onions develop best when they have plenty of light and air. It's a good idea to pull weeds out by hand around onions to avoid the possibility of heaping dirt around the growing plants.*

BULBING ONIONS

PLANT in early spring as soon as the soil can be worked. Sow at ½" depth in rows 18" apart, pressing soil firmly over seeds.
THIN to 3" apart when seedlings are about 3" high. Thinnings are delicious.

KNOCK DOWN TOPS at the bulb neck when bulbs are fully mature (in fall before first freeze). This allows bulbs to ripen and dry off at the top for better storage.

PULL BULBS out of the ground and leave on surface to dry for a few days. Store in cool, ventilated place.

PARSLEY

This native of the Mediterranean area has been used as a garnish and seasoning for thousands of years. The ancient Greeks and Romans thought that by eating parsley you could keep from getting drunk. It was also used in festive garlands and as a decoration for tombs because of its ability to stay green indefinitely.

Parsley's crisp green leaves and distinctive taste make it a popular addition to salads, stuffings, meat dishes, soups and sauces. Many cooks sprinkle it on boiled or mashed potatoes.

There are two kinds of parsley: the familiar curled variety used most often as a garnish, and the flat-leaved Italian type favored for cooking.

Full sunlight isn't essential for parsley, and it can stand heavy frost.

SOAK SEEDS in warm water for 24 hours before planting to aid germination, which is slow — 18 to 24 days.

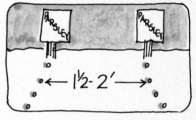

PLANT in rich, moist soil. Scatter seed thinly ¼" deep in rows 1½ to 2 feet apart. Press soil firmly over seeds.

THIN to 4" apart in row. Harvest as needed. Cut stems with a sharp knife and the plant will keep on producing.

DIG UP a clump in the fall and place it indoors in a sunny window. Besides adding a decorative note, it will provide garnishes all winter.

PARSNIPS

Everyone seems to have a very definite opinion about parsnips — you either love them or you hate them. Much of the antipathy toward parsnips arises from the fact that parsnips must be picked and eaten at their peak to be enjoyable; otherwise they develop a rather disagreeable texture and flavor.

Boiled or french fried, a dish of home-grown parsnips picked at maximum flavor is a gourmet's delight.

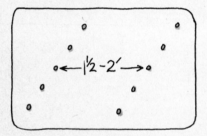

PLANT in rich, loamy soil that has been deeply spaded. Scatter seed sparingly in rows 1½ to 2 feet apart. Cover with ½'' of tamped soil.

CULTIVATE soon after seedlings appear (about 2-3 weeks). Soil should be kept moist throughout germination period.

THIN seedlings when they are 2 or 3 inches tall to about a 3'' spacing.

HARVEST as late as you wish; freezing actually improves the flavor. Many gardeners leave some roots in garden right over the winter.

PEAS

The pea gets its name from the Latin *pisum*, which became "pease" in medieval England. Many people thought pease was plural, so it wasn't long before the singular became "pea." Archaeologists have found seeds of primitive pea varieties in Europe that date back 5,000 years or so, but garden peas did not become common until the 18th century. Before that they were prized by gourmets as a rare delicacy. In fact, during the late 17th century over-indulgence in peas was often cited as one of the extravagant excesses of the French court of Louis XIV.

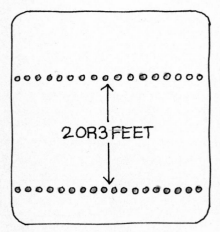

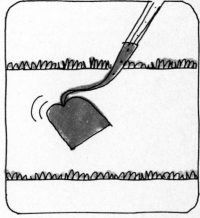

PLANT in very early spring. Sow seeds about 2" apart in furrows spaced 2 to 3 feet apart. Cover about 1½" deep. Firm the soil well over the seeds.

CULTIVATE soon after seedlings appear (6 to 10 days). Shallow hoeing is best.

At first, peas were cooked in their pods and licked out at the table. The English later developed the technique of eating peas with a knife. Many people nowadays prefer the new edible-podded varieties such as Dwarf Gray Sugar or Chinese Edible Pod, which are picked young and eaten pod and all.

Peas are a good source of Vitamins A, B, C, and G. They are easy to prepare: just simmer them for 12 to 15 minutes. Cook a few mint leaves with peas for a special treat. Basil, dill, marjoram, oregano, rosemary, poppy seed, sage and savory will also give peas an interesting flavor.

CANNING: Wash freshly-picked peas thoroughly, then drain and shell. Boil 3 to 5 minutes and follow usual canning procedure.

FREEZING: Choose only tender, mature peas. Shell and scald for two minutes, then chill in cold water and freeze. Don't delay between shelling and freezing or skins will toughen.

HOW MUCH TO PLANT: About 12 feet of row per person will produce an adequate supply. Plant more if you plan to can or freeze.

HARVEST when the pods are well filled. Don't delay picking mature peas; hot weather can carry them past their peak very quickly.

HARVESTING TIP: Hold the vine while picking to prevent damage.

PEPPERS

Don't confuse the pepper you grow in your garden with the pepper you use for seasoning. When Columbus found the West Indian natives growing a hot-tasting vegetable, he thought he had found one of the spices he was seeking on his voyage, and he named it "pepper." Our garden pepper is actually not related at all to the true pepper used as a table condiment.

There are many varieties of garden peppers — pimiento, cayenne, chili, paprika — but the large-fruited sweet pepper is the favorite of most American gardeners. Cooked or eaten raw in salads and sandwiches, peppers have a distinctive flavor that blends well with other foods. They are usually eaten in their immature green stage, but are also delicious after they have fully ripened and turned red or yellow. They are especially rich in Vitamin A; a single pepper will provide twice the recommended daily minimum.

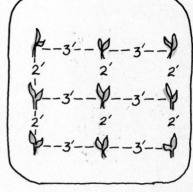

PLANT seed indoors and transplant after soil and weather have warmed up. Choose the sunniest part of your garden.

SET TRANSPLANTS every 2 feet in rows 3 feet apart. (Seed may be started outdoors in warm areas — see map and chart on Pages 16-17.)

A favorite dish in American homes is peppers stuffed with rice and meat or seafood. Peppers also give a zesty flavor to soups and stews. They will retain their fresh flavor in the refrigerator for three to five days after picking.

CANNING: Use either green or red peppers. Wash and drain, remove stems and seeds, then boil for three minutes and follow usual canning procedure.

FREEZING: Remove seeds and inner white ribs from peppers, cut into strips, and freeze in usual way. No blanching is necessary.

HOW MUCH TO PLANT: About 6 feet of row will supply one person well. Plant more if you plan to can or freeze.

WHEN TO PLANT: Peppers are native to the sub-tropics, so be sure all danger of frost is past before moving transplants outdoors.

HARVESTING TIPS: Peppers will store better if you leave ½" of stem on. When they are firm to the touch, peppers are ready to pick.

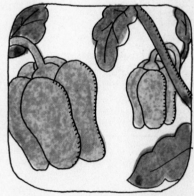

THIN direct-seeded plants when about 2 inches tall; space every two feet.

HARVEST only when the fruit is mature; unlike other vegetables, the tiny peppers aren't very good. Pick off mature fruit to keep plant producing.

POTATOES

It takes a large amount of space to raise a good crop of potatoes, but many home gardeners plant a few in order to enjoy the superb taste of tiny young potatoes.

This is one vegetable you won't find on the seed racks. For best results in growing potatoes it's necessary to buy seed potatoes, which are specially selected and certified free of disease. Cut each seed potato into egg-size chunks, making sure each chunk has one or two "eyes" (miniature buds) on it. Let the chunks stand at least 24 hours before planting.

PLANT when the soil is warm and dry, placing each seed chunk about 5" deep with the eyes up. Mound soil around each one.

CULTIVATE no deeper than 1" to avoid damaging sprouting plants.

AS PLANTS DEVELOP, protect the young tubers by mounding the surrounding soil around each plant to a height of 4-5".

HARVEST at varying stages of development. Decide for yourself the size and flavor you like best.

PUMPKIN

Besides being the source of memorable pie fillings, the pumpkin is the traditional symbol of fall and harvest time in America. And at Halloween, of course, weird and wonderful pumpkin faces appear on porches and in windows of homes everywhere.

The pumpkin is really a member of the squash family, and the instructions for planting winter squash (pages 54-55) apply to pumpkins as well. Many home gardeners, however, like to concentrate their pumpkin-growing efforts on producing a single mammoth pumpkin. Here's how to go about it:

Pick off all but one seedling in a hill, then fertilize it weekly. In early summer, pick off all but the one largest fruit on the plant retained. All the nutriment intended for the entire hill of pumpkins will go to that one remaining fruit; you'll probably wind up with a "bragging-type" pumpkin.

HARVESTING TIP: When the pumpkin is fully matured, cut it off the vine, leaving a stem attached, and allow it to stand in the garden for a few days to let the skin harden.

RADISHES

How would you like to see a 100-pound radish in your garden? One of that size was reported by a German botanist in 1544. But modern varieties range only from marble-size to some of the Oriental radishes that achieve basketball size.

Radishes grow best in cool weather with full sun, but high temperatures may give them a somewhat peppery flavor. Thinning is especially important with radishes; if crowded they will fail to bulb and go all to tops. Plant in early spring as soon as the ground can be worked. Make successive plantings 2 weeks apart for a continuous supply.

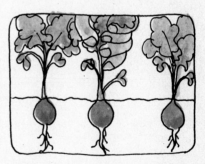

SOW thinly ¼" deep in rows 1 to 2 feet apart. Press soil firmly over seed. Thin several times until plants are 1" apart in the rows.

HARVEST as soon as they reach eating size for best flavor and crispness. If you wait too long they turn pithy and strong.

SQUASH

There are two principal types of squash grown by home gardeners. *Summer squash* is the small, fast-growing kind that you harvest in midsummer and eat while the rinds are still soft (Crookneck, Straightneck, Bush Scallop, Cocozelle, Zucchini). This is the most prolific vegetable you can plant. If you keep the fruit picked off your summer squash will keep producing prodigiously until fall frost.

Winter squash is the hard-rind type, often warty and odd-shaped (Hubbard, Butternut, Buttercup, Acorn, Banana). This type you harvest later in the season. It is usually served baked or steamed in half shell. Winter squash stores well for months.

Both kinds are native to the Western Hemisphere; the word squash itself comes from the Indian word *askutasquash*. That translates as "eaten raw," but you'll probably prefer cooked squash. However, adventurous cooks report that at least one of the squash varieties, Zucchini, is delicious served raw in finger-size slices and as a substitute for cucumbers in salads.

The summer varieties are easiest to prepare for cooking. Just wash and slice or dice them into proper-size pieces and they're ready for boiling, baking or panning. Summer squash cooks in its own juice in just a few minutes; there's no need to add any water at all. Served with onion, butter, salt and pepper, it's a gourmet's delight. Here's another favorite recipe of squash enthusiasts:

BAKED SUMMER SQUASH

Place three pounds of squash (sliced ½" thick) in a casserole, dot with butter or margarine, sprinkle with salt and one tablespoon finely-chopped onion. Add a little water and cover. Bake in 400° oven until squash is tender (50 minutes to one hour).

CANNING: Winter squash is preferred for canning. Steam or bake large pieces after removing seeds. When tender, pulp is scooped out, cooled and put through a food mill. Add boiling water to make consistency a little thinner than pie mix. Follow usual canning procedure.

FREEZING: Summer squash — Blanch 1" slices for 2-3 minutes, then chill in cold water and freeze. *Winter squash* — Bake or steam large pieces after removing seeds. When tender, pulp is scooped out and cooled. Freeze in usual way.

HOW MUCH TO PLANT: About two plants of summer squash or four plants of winter squash per person will be adequate.

HARVESTING TIPS: Basically the winter squash is ripe when it's hard to the fingernail. Pick with part of the stem, being careful to avoid any bruising. Summer squash is best when about 4-6" long, with soft rind.

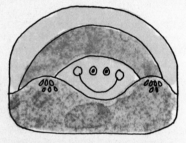

PLANT in well-drained, moderately rich soil in full sunlight. *Summer squash:* put 6 to 8 seeds 1" deep in hills 4 to 6 feet apart. Or plant seeds 4" apart in rows 4 feet apart. *Winter squash:* increase row spacing to 6-8 feet.

CULTIVATE when the seedlings appear (this should be in 6 to 10 days). Shallow cultivation will produce best results.

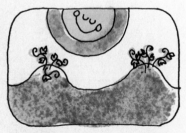

THIN plants when they reach 2" in height. Thin gradually until you have one healthy plant every 3 or 4 feet. Thin hill-type plantings to best 3 or 4 plants in each hill.

HARVEST your summer squash when they are still small and tender, before the rind hardens. Pick winter squash only after rind becomes hard in late summer or fall.

TOMATO

Would you believe that at one time most Americans thought the tomato was poisonous? It's strange but true. Somehow the idea took root in this country that the tomato, being a member of the poisonous Nightshade family, was lethal itself. It was grown here as an ornamental garden plant (called the "love apple") but few Americans dared to eat it. Toward the middle of the 19th century this odd notion was gradually dispelled and the tomato finally took its place as one of our most popular vegetables.

Tomato recipes abound everywhere, since tomatoes can be eaten raw or cooked; as a main or side dish; in soups, stews, or meatloaves; baked, fried, stuffed, canned or pickled. Housewives have only one complaint about tomatoes: they don't freeze well. Frozen tomatoes usually thaw to a mushy state that bears no relationship to the firm, flavorsome fruit you pick off the vine; they make good flavoring for soups and stews, however.

TOMATO JUICE with just-picked flavor is easy for home gardeners. Boil tomatoes in their own juice for a few minutes, then run through a food mill to remove seeds and skin. Add salt and sugar to taste.

PLANT seed indoors, transplanting after both soil and weather have warmed up. (Seed may be started outdoors in warm areas — see map and chart on Pages 16-17.)

SET TRANSPLANTS every 3 to 4 feet. Cultivate as weeds appear; shallow hoeing is best.

HOW MUCH TO PLANT: Plan on 3 to 4 tomato plants for each person, although harvests vary greatly with tomatoes depending on fertilizing, moisture and weather conditions. Plant more if you plan to can or make juice of the surplus.

WHEN TO PLANT: Tomatoes are very sensitive to cold; be sure all frost danger is past before planting seeds or moving transplant seedlings outdoors.

HARVESTING TIPS: Pick tomatoes when fully ripe for best flavor. Then just before the first fall frost, pick all the green tomatoes on your vines. Wrap each one in paper and store in the dark at about 55°F. They will gradually ripen. Or you can use the green tomatoes in dozens of other ways — canned, pickled, fried, in relishes or spreads, in catsup, or even in pies and cookies.

SHOULD YOU STAKE YOUR TOMATOES? Staking is a popular practice because staked tomatoes are cleaner and easier to pick. But there are fewer tomatoes per plant and staked tomatoes seem to crack and get sunscalded more easily. If you stake your tomatoes, pick off suckers when they are 2 to 4 inches long. (A sucker is a shoot that appears in the V's formed by stems off the main stalk.) Many gardeners mulch under their tomatoes to give fruit a cushion on which to ripen.

DON'T OVERWATER TOMATOES — This can cause the fruit to crack. Or you could cut off the oxygen supply to the roots and literally suffocate the plant.

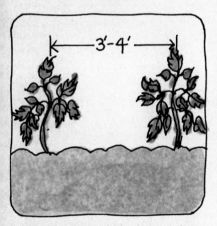

THIN direct-seeded plants when about 2" tall; space to 3 or 4 feet apart.

HARVEST mature fruit regularly; this will increase harvest and eliminate undesirable rotting of fruit on the vine.

TURNIP

This hardy vegetable developed in the Mediterranean area and has served mankind well over the centuries. It has been used as a staple food for both humans and animals, as a remedy for gout, and as a cosmetic aid. In the days of Henry VIII, English families would boil or bake the turnip roots, cook the tops as greens, and serve up the young shoots as a salad.

The turnip provides a prime example of the great difference in flavor that home gardening can bring to your table. The mild, sweet flavor of a young turnip comes as a pleasant surprise to anyone accustomed to the strong, often bitter taste of overly mature turnips.

Turnips are a good source of vitamins, especially the greens which are rich in Vitamins A and C. Cooking is very simple; turnips can be boiled, creamed, baked, glazed, or added to soups or stews. Boiled turnip greens are delicious; in fact, one variety (Seven Top) is raised for its greens alone.

CANNING: Wash and cut freshly-dug turnips into medium-size pieces. Boil 3 minutes and follow usual canning procedure. (Note: Canned turnips usually develop a stronger flavor and discolor somewhat.)

FREEZING: Remove tops, wash, peel and cut into small chunks. Scald for two minutes, chill, and freeze.

WHEN TO PLANT: Get the seeds in as soon as the ground can be worked in the spring; turnips are very hardy and thrive in cool temperatures. For a winter crop, plant in late summer or even in early fall.

PLANT in light, well-drained soil, placing seeds ½" deep in rows 1 to 2 feet apart. Firm soil well over seeds.

CULTIVATE soon after seedlings appear (4 to 7 days).

THIN plants when they are 2 to 3 inches high. Do your thinning gradually, until plants are 3 to 4 inches apart. Greens are ready for eating after 30 days or so. (Do not thin if you are raising turnips for greens.)

HARVEST when root is about 2 inches in diameter for best flavor. Plants may be left in the ground until freeze-up if you desire.

STIR-FRYING is growing in popularity with adventurous cooks, and it brings especially delightful results with your fresh-from-the-garden produce. This Chinese method of hot-oil cooking is easiest with the traditional "wok," a cast-iron frypan with sloping sides, but it can also be done with an electric frypan or heavy skillet.

Cut your favorite vegetables into thin strips; tear leafy greens into large pieces. Get three tablespoons of vegetable or olive oil piping hot in your cooking vessel, then put in the vegetable slices. Start tossing and turning, and keep it up until the vegetables are cooked tender — not more than four minutes or so. Remember that stir-frying requires ultra-thin slices (matchstick thickness) and oil that is extremely hot — almost smoking.

CANNING TIPS: Let your garden plan your canning schedule for you — it's much more fun to process just a few jars at a time. Pick each vegetable at its peak of flavor, can it quickly, and you'll enjoy months — even years — of good eating.

Avoid "short-cut" canning methods . . . follow traditional canning methods for safest results. And remember, a cool, dark, dry storage area will help keep your canned vegetables at their tastiest.

A WORD ABOUT FREEZING VEGETABLES . . .

The combination of a home garden and a freezer will produce month after month of vegetable delights for your table. Pick your vegetables at their peak of flavor and texture; freezing will retain much of this freshly-harvested goodness. It's a smart idea to blanch most vegetables to extend their storage life. After blanching, chill in running cold water. Drain and pack in moistureproof packages, then freeze immediately. Vegetables will store well for a year or more if you keep your freezer at 0° or lower. Above that temperature, vegetables lose quality rapidly even though they may appear solidly frozen.

Gardener's Dictionary

APHIDS. Also called plant lice, these are small, soft-bodied insects that suck the sap out of plant cells, causing discoloration of foliage, curling of leaves and blighting of harvests. Usually green, but some are brown, yellow, pink or black.

AVAILABILITY. This is a term used in connection with plant food, and indicates whether the food is in a form the plant can use. In most chemical fertilizers the nutrients are immediately available; in the natural fertilizers, bacterial action gradually makes the nutrients available.

BLANCHING. Whitening the leaves or stems of plants by excluding light. Celery and endive gardeners blanch the plant's inner leaves to make them more tender by tying up the coarser outer leaves. (Do not confuse with blanching as a cooking term.)

CHLOROSIS. Yellowing of foliage caused by a lack of chlorophyll. This is usually induced by a minerals deficiency, excessive soil alkalinity, or lack of moisture.

CLAY SOIL. This is soil with very fine particles (less than 0.002 mm in diameter). Clay soil holds moisture tenaciously and takes a long time to dry out.

CLONE. A variety of plants created by grafting or budding rather than from seed.

COLD FRAME. A miniature "greenhouse" built right in the garden area for early starting of plants.

COMPOST. Rich, loose rotted organic material valuable for soil preparation and fertilizing. (See Page 31.)

COVER CROP. A fast-growing crop (ryegrass, for instance) that is plowed under to enrich the soil as it decays and forms humus. Can also be legumes or other crops left all season and turned under in the fall.

CUCURBIT. Any member of the gourd family (pumpkins, squash, cucumber, melons, etc.).

CULTIVAR. A cultivated variety, developed by plant breeding or selection, which differs from its original botanical species.

CUTWORMS. Hungry caterpillars that spend the winter as moth larvae and emerge in the spring to eat tender young plants, cutting them off at ground level. Can be foiled by protecting stems with collars of paper or other material extending 2" above and 2" below ground level.

DAMPING OFF. A fungus disease that kills off tender young plants just as they emerge. Usually caused by too thick planting, high heat and humidity. Can be prevented by sterilizing soil (see Page 12).

DIBBER. Pointed tool used to make holes in soft soil for setting plants. Also called a "dibble."

DORMANCY. A rest period taken by plants during unfavorable environmental conditions (cold, drought, heat). Some plants will take an occasional rest period even when conditions are ideal, probably a holdover from their original life cycle.

EARLY. This has two meanings for gardeners. An early *variety* is one that matures fast. An early *crop* is one you plant early in the season.

FERTILIZER BURN. Damage caused by applying dry commercial fertilizer directly to foliage or roots.

FILLER. Inert material used for bulk in fertilizers or soil conditioners.

FUNGICIDE. A compound used to kill plant fungi that cause disease.

GERMINATION. Changing the dormant state of seed into growth. Most seeds begin sprouting under the right conditions of temperature, moisture and oxygen, but there is a tremendous variation in germination time among various species.

HARDENING OFF. Toughening of seedlings grown indoors by gradual exposure to the conditions they will encounter outdoors.

HARDPAN. Layer of impervious soil just below the topsoil which must be broken up to enable roots to go deep down.

HEAVY SOIL. A dense clay soil that resists working. Refers to consistency, not weight. Granular, porous, sandy soil that's easy to work is called "light."

HERBICIDE. Compound used to kill weeds.

HOTBED. Similar to cold frame, but artificially heated.

HUMUS. Decomposed remains of vegetable and animal matter in soil that adds valuable nutrients, improves soil texture, holds moisture and provides a good environment for bacterial growth beneficial to the soil.

INBREEDING. System used in developing hybrid varieties wherein pollination is carefully controlled to develop a line with uniformity and predictable characteristics.

INSECTICIDE. Preparation used to kill insects.

LEAF MOLD. Decayed leaves, helpful as a soil additive but of little nutritive value.

LEGGY. Term used to describe vegetable plants grown with too much heat or nutrients, making them tall and slender with weak stems. Can also be caused by lack of light due to crowding or shady location.

LOAM. A soil mixture somewhere between clay and sand which contains organic matter and is usually considered ideal for gardening.

MANURE. Animal and vegetable matter used to enrich the soil; in this country, usually applied to animal excrement.

MOSAIC. Diseases that result in uneven coloration of leaves. Usually caused by viruses.

MULCH. Loose layer of dead organic material that serves as a protective covering over soil. (See Page 15.)

NURSE CROP. Sturdy plants grown simultaneously with less rugged varieties to protect them during germination stages.

ORGANIC GARDENING. Using natural methods of fertilizing, insect control and soil enrichment. (See Page 15.)

PEAT MOSS. Partially-decomposed plant life taken from bogs and used as a rooting medium, soil conditioner or mulch.

PERLITE. A commercial product made from volcanic material and used in the same way as peat moss.

pH. Scientific rating scale from 0 to 14 used to indicate the acidity/alkalinity level of soil. A pH rating of 7 is neutral. Lower readings indicate acid soil; higher readings indicate alkaline.

PHOTOPERIODISM. The effect of varying daylight length on plants. A timing mechanism in plants responds to varying periods of daylight to trigger various plant reactions.

POTHERB. Any plant you raise for its greens.

POTTING MIXTURE. A combination of soil and other rooting media (peat, sand, perlite, vermiculite) designed to give transplants or indoor plants the ideal conditions for growth.

PUDDLING. Dipping roots of transplants into a slurry made of soil and water. Prevents roots from drying out during transplanting process.

ROGUEING. Removal of undesirable, inferior or off-type plants from a planting.

RUST. Diseases caused by fungi and recognized by the iron rust color they give to plants.

SALT HAY. Hay cut on salt marshes near the oceans and valued for mulching because it is free from weed seeds and has a stiff quality that minimizes matting down.

SCALE INSECT. Sedentary tough-shelled sucking insect that feeds on plant juices.

SET. Undersized bulb (of onions, for instance) grown to be used the following season for early planting.

SHEET COMPOSTING. Applying compost materials directly to the garden instead of using a compost pile.

SILT. A soil type that is somewhere between sand and clay in particle size (0.002 to 0.005 mm).

SPHAGNUM. A light inert moss that eventually decomposes into peat moss.

TILTH. A way of describing the "feel" of soil. The right proportions of sand, clay and fillers will produce soil with a "good tilth."

VARIETY. A group of closely-related plants below the level of species, all of which share certain characteristics. Usually developed by breeding or selection.

VERMICULITE. A lightweight commercial rooting medium or soil additive made of expanded mica.

INDEX

(Bold-face number indicates main listing for subject.)

Every step to successful gardening — planning and planting, care and feeding, even how to cook what you grow — in one illustrated, easy-to-understand book. **PLUS** Special Bicentennial Section on Pumpkins, Pumpkin Recipes and Colonial Gardening! For your copy, send coupon and **$1.00** (no stamps, please) to:

Gardening Guide, Box 797, Maple Plain, Minnesota 55359.

Name _____
            (please print)

Address _____

City _____ State _____ Zip _____

While supply lasts. Void where prohibited, taxed or regulated. Allow 4 weeks for delivery.

NK Northrup King's **Basic Vegetable Gardening Guide.**

Every step to successful gardening — planning and planting, care and feeding, even how to cook what you grow — in one illustrated, easy-to-understand book. **PLUS** Special Bicentennial Section on Pumpkins, Pumpkin Recipes and Colonial Gardening! For your copy, send coupon and **$1.00** (no stamps, please) to:

Gardening Guide, Box 797, Maple Plain, Minnesota 55359.

Name _____
            (please print)

Address _____

City _____ State _____ Zip _____

While supply lasts. Void where prohibited, taxed or regulated. Allow 4 weeks for delivery.